The Litt'
of Woo

by Terry Gould and Linda Mort
Illustrations by Mike Phillips

LITTLE BOOKS WITH BIG IDEAS

Published 2012 by Featherstone Education, an imprint of Bloomsbury Publishing plc
50 Bedford Square, London, WC1B 3DP
www.bloomsbury.com

ISBN 978-1-4081-7396-1

Printed in Great Britain by Latimer Trend & Company Limited
10 9 8 7 6 5 4 3 2 1
This book is produced using paper that is made from wood grown in
managed, sustainable forests. It is natural, renewable and recyclable.

The logging and manufacturing processes conform to the environmental
regulations of the country of origin.

**To see our full range of titles
visit www.bloomsbury.com**

Contents

Introduction

Foreword

In the 1950s, when I was a young child, woodwork benches in nurseries were much more common than they are today. However, I went to a nursery which had no woodwork bench. I really envied my best friend, Jeffrey, who attended a different nursery and was always talking excitedly about 'hammerin' and 'nailin'. He would proudly show me his 'machines' – lots of pieces of wood nailed together – as well as his more recognisable 'boats and aeroplanes'.

At secondary school, my very first woodwork class was memorable – for all the wrong reasons. As I inexpertly tapped away at a piece of wood, the teacher bellowed at me: 'Stop that, boy! That is parana pine!' Totally ignorant about wood, I thought he had said 'piranha' and had a fearsome vision of a ravenous fish gobbling up my fingers for lunch! After this dramatic introduction, the world of woodwork and I went our separate ways.

Jeffrey and I both became language teachers and, over half a century later, we are still friends but, whereas I am incapable of putting up even a simple shelf, he positively relishes every DIY challenge. Nothing fazes him; he just says 'I'll find a way!' And he always does. A few years ago he virtually built, single-handed, his own house!

How I wish **The Little Book of Woodwork** had been around to inspire my nursery teachers! The book is clearly set out and reassuring, with 'do-able' suggestions which leave scope for children's creativity. I feel sure it will help to create a new generation of problem-solvers who, like Jeffrey, will find their way confidently with wood, and in life.

David Mort, May 2012

Why provide woodworking experiences in the early years?

"Woodworking in early years settings fosters creativity and problem solving" (Moorhouse, Peter 2012) [1] 'What a child can do safely with adult support today they can do safely for themselves tomorrow'. So using woodworking tools is about learning across all 7 areas of learning and development. Subject to appropriate risk assessments and children having been taught how to use them safely, woodworking tools can be used with young children in the same way as scissors, glue, staplers and hole punches. Indeed the government review of health and safety laws, 'Common Sense, Common Safety' [2] (September, 2010) has encouraged a positive change of outlook from 'risk-aversion' assessment to 'risk-benefit' assessment.

It is important to recognise that many woodworking activities already take place safely in a wide range of settings – including those which provide forest school type experiences. These settings demonstrate that woodworking in the early years, when appropriately provided, is a very valuable activity for all children because it:

▶ enables children to purposefully create with natural materials and in this way connect with the natural world

▶ supports the use of a range of tools with growing confidence, expertise and safety and develops both gross and fine motor skills

▶ develops important and significant language, listening, thinking and communication skills

▶ builds up children's levels of perseverance and self-esteem through a sense of satisfaction and enjoyment in their achievement

▶ develops a range of social skills including developing independence, a sense of pride and responsibility associated with using real tools, turn-taking and collaborative work

▶ develops and supports children's key problem solving and self reflection skills

▶ enables children to engage through the full age range of learning styles including kinaesthetic, auditory and visual. (In this aspect it is particularly valuable to boys' but also to girls' learning.)

▶ is cross-curricular in its nature (covers prime and specific areas of learning)

Links to the prime and specific areas of learning and development (EYFS 2012)

All the activities in this book are based on ideas that support the prime and specific areas of the revised EYFS:

PRIME AREAS

Physical Development

- ▶ Develop hand-eye coordination
- ▶ Develop small scale spatial awareness
- ▶ Develop fine motor skills
- ▶ Learn to handle tools safely and with increasing control
- ▶ Develop awareness of the safe use of space and the needs of others

Communication and Language

- ▶ Talk about and discuss their thoughts and ideas
- ▶ Learn a range of new and descriptive vocabulary
- ▶ Listen and respond to things they hear such as instructions and safety advice

Personal, Social and Emotional Development

- ▶ Build self-esteem and confidence in using woodworking tools and skills
- ▶ Improve concentration and perseverance skills
- ▶ Work alone or with others
- ▶ Have suitable opportunities for independence
- ▶ Be more motivated to engage in learning
- ▶ Understand about their own and others' need for safety
- ▶ Able to make their own choices

SPECIFIC AREAS

Through a focus on being creative and developing knowledge, skills and understanding within aspects of the specific areas of:

Understanding the World

- ▶ Find out about the properties of wood and tools and other resources
- ▶ Learn about what things can be used for

Mathematics

▶ Begin to think more closely about the relationship of size and shape

▶ Measure and make things to size and sometimes in proportion

Expressive Arts and Design

▶ Learn about new ways to be creative, imaginative and expressive

▶ Explore and combine materials

▶ Find enjoyment and intrinsic fulfilment in the creative process

Literacy

▶ Design, make, and write instructions and engage in creative writing and mark-making

▶ Create labelled drawings and make group/class books about things they have made.

Safety as a priority

When starting to provide woodworking experiences in a setting ensuring that the activities can take place safely must be a priority. This means that:

▶ children need the task at hand carefully explained to them (then reminded several times!).

▶ it must be emphasised that tools are not toys and practitioners must give appropriate guidance and support on how the tools should be used. In our experience children will 'rise to the occasion' and respond well to the fact that they are being trusted to use real tools.

▶ initially there needs to be close support and supervision until practitioners are fully satisfied that children know how to use the tools appropriately and safely.

Practitioners should observe how children's skills are developing and use this to plan the next steps using the **observational based assessment cycle for learning and development**:

▶ Observe and share what you observe

▶ Think and assess

▶ Plan and decide what next

▶ Provide and respond

(Further detailed guidance on '**closely matching what they provide to a child's current needs**' is provided in **Development Matters** (Early Education Page 4, March 2012)

Risk Assessment

All settings should have a risk assessment policy in place which will consider the appropriate and safe use of a wide range of resources and tools such as scissors, pencils, glue etc. Using woodwork related tools and resources requires similar consideration. Tools used by children for woodworking must be real and of an appropriate size for the children to use them safely and purposefully.

Some top safety tips for woodworking activities:

▶ Always talk to the children about the tools and resources and model their use.

▶ Use planed, softwood timber e.g. pine and avoid the use of hardwoods; Hardwoods are not really suitable for sawing, drilling and hammering by children at this age.

▶ Always use real tools (not toys), of an appropriate size for your children to hold.

▶ Explain to the children, and discuss with them the differences between pretend tools and the real ones they are using in their woodwork.

▶ Safety goggles and protective aprons should be worn as and when practitioner feels is appropriate.

▶ Introduce the tools and resources gradually over a period of time, using observations of individual children's levels of competence to inform the next steps.

▶ Regularly check the tools to ensure they are in safe working order.

▶ Set up some simple, child-friendly basic rules to follow, including the return of tools to their labelled storage place.

▶ Keep the area as dust free as possible by regularly brushing up any sawdust and off-cuts, etc.

▶ When sawing ensure the children wear a suitably protective glove on their free hand – keeping this hand away from mishaps with the saw!

▶ Using a dust mask will be a consideration if any of the children are asthmatic.

▶ Settings should begin woodworking activities with a higher than usual adult to child ratio and then reduce this ratio as children's levels of confidence and skills develop.

► In the early stages the use of a mini awl by the adult can be used to start off holes in the wood, before children start hammering in nails.

► Adults can use a saw to prepare off-cuts by pre-cutting them into workable shapes and sizes before giving them to the children.

Differentiated levels of ability and level-appropriate tools

This book supports practitioners in choosing the right types of tools and resources and gives ideas and examples of the types of experiences that you can easily provide in your setting. The suggestions in this book are not intended to be prescriptive, but rather as descriptions of simple 'how to' skills that can be applied to a wide range of woodworking experiences. Practitioners are encouraged to be creative in the experiences they provide and to use these ideas as a basis of creating their own and children's ideas.

Recommendation

Where practitioners have not had the experience of working in a setting in which high quality woodwork experiences are provided then it is very worthwhile for them to visit a setting where woodworking is successfully taking place. By seeing the provision in action they will be inspired and reassured!

To ensure that the differentiation of skills is appropriate for the developmental stage of the children in your setting, this book provides ideas within four progressive levels of difficulty and challenge. Each of the four sections starts with an outline of the types of tools and equipment that will be used within the activities provided in this level. As these levels are about stages of development (not age) we have not put any ages against these levels.

Our identified four levels are:

(A) Beginner level

(B) Emerging skills level

(C) Developing competence level

(D) Advanced competence level

We both believe that woodworking experiences should be provided for young children and we hope that this book will inspire others to share our passion and use it to develop outcomes for children's learning on all levels.

Terry Gould and Linda Mort, August 2012

(A) Beginner level

Tools and other resources required for this level

▶ child-sized small hammers – those without 'claws'

▶ sanding blocks (ready made with a flexible, foam based centre)

▶ appropriately sized, chunky, woodworking pencils

▶ small variety of nails with suitably large round and flat heads ideally between 30mm-50mm in length

▶ masking tape or suitable alternative

▶ PVA glue in squeezy container and glue spreaders

ALL TOOLS SHOULD BE STORED IN A SAFE BUT ACCESSIBLE WAY E.G. USING SILHOUTTES ON SHELVES OR ON A RACK.

Hammering into clay

What you need:

► child-sized hammers
► clay
► woodworking bench (or suitable table)
► small wooden boards (to place the clay on)
► small modelling tools (optional)

What you do:

► Provide each child with a medium-sized lump of clay, a board and a hammer.

► On a workbench, model and explain the safe way to use the hammer to gently hammer the clay.

► Support the children in practising safe use of the hammer. First, allow the children free use of the hammers with the clay. Then ask the children to mark a spot on the clay (with a small modelling tool or similar) and aim at the mark with the hammer.

► Ask the children to replace the hammers appropriately at the end of the activity.

Key vocabulary and questions

► clay, hammer, hammering, flatten, mark
► Can you hammer the clay?
► What is happening to the clay as you hammer it?

Safety issues

► Show the children how to use the hammer safely and correctly – model and give guidance several times.

► Ensure the children are not too close to each other – talk to them about this. Make sure any left-handed child is not right next to a right-handed child.

► Remind the children how to store the hammers correctly after use.

Hammering golf tees into clay

What you need:

- ▶ child-sized hammers
- ▶ blocks of fresh clay cut into suitably sized pieces
- ▶ small wooden boards
- ▶ variety of plastic golf tees
- ▶ small modelling tools
- ▶ woodworking bench

I will need

What you do:

▶ Provide a suitably sized block of clay, a hammer and up to 20 plastic golf tees for each child. The clay should be in blocks which are deeper than the length of the tees.

▶ Model the activity for the children and explain the safe use of the hammer and the tees.

▶ Support the children in hammering tees freely into the clay, first with adult support and then independently.

▶ Move the children on to mark a spot on the clay (e.g. with a cross) using a small modelling tool or similar then ask them to aim and hammer the tee into that mark on the clay.

▶ Ask the children if they can get the tees out of the clay. Observe what strategies they use to do this.

Key vocabulary and questions

▶ clay, hammer, hammering, mark, golf, name of colours

▶ Can you hammer the tee into clay?

▶ What is happening to the tee when you hammer it into clay?

Safety issues

▶ Show children how to use the hammer and tees safely and correctly – give guidance several times.

▶ Ensure children are not too close to each other.

▶ Show the correct storage of the hammers after use.

Sanding a piece of wood

What you need:

- ▶ flexible sanding blocks
- ▶ off-cuts of planed soft timber in a range of sizes (for children to choose from)
- ▶ safety masks (for asthmatic children)

I will need

What you do:

▶ Let each child choose a piece of planed softwood and a sanding block.

▶ Model the activity for the children and explain the safe use of the sanding block.

▶ Support children using the sanding block to make the wood surface smooth.

▶ Provide free use of the sanding block on the wooden off-cuts.

▶ Suggest parts of the wood to focus on e.g. corners, edges, flat surfaces.

Key vocabulary and questions

▶ sanding block, wood, smooth, rough, corner, edge, surface, flat surfaces

▶ Can you make all the wood surfaces and edges smooth?

▶ What is happening to the wood as you sand it?

Safety issues

▶ Show children how to use the sanding block safely and correctly – give guidance several times.

▶ Remind the children of the correct storage of the sanding blocks after use.

▶ If any child is asthmatic consider providing a safety mask for them to wear.

Hammering nails into a foam block

What you need:

- small child-sized hammers
- rigid foam blocks
- large round head nails approx. 30mm long
- workbench (or suitable table)

What you do:

▶ Provide each child with a foam block, a hammer and nails.

▶ Model the activity for the children.

▶ Show the correct and safe use of hammering the head of the nail to drive it into the foam block.

▶ Support independent hammering of the nails into the block.

N.B. Adults will later need to remove the nails from the blocks using pliers.

Key vocabulary and questions

▶ nails, head, hammer in, foam block

▶ Can you make the nail go into the block?

▶ What is happening to the nail when you hammer it?

Safety issues

▶ Show children how to safely and correctly hammer the nail – model and give guidance several times.

▶ Ensure children are not too close to each other.

▶ Remind children about the correct storage of tools, remaining nails and foam blocks after use.

Hammering into a log slice

What you need:

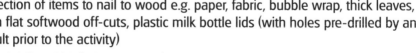

- ▶ slices of soft log
- ▶ child-sized hammers
- ▶ a range of large roundhead nails (approx. 20mm-50mm long)
- ▶ selection of items to nail to wood e.g. paper, fabric, bubble wrap, thick leaves, thin flat softwood off-cuts, plastic milk bottle lids (with holes pre-drilled by an adult prior to the activity)
- ▶ hand drill and bit (adult use only)

What you do:

▶ Provide the hammers, log slices, thin flat softwood off-cuts, nails, paper, card, etc. for children to select.

▶ Encourage children to hammer nails and their choice of the items provided into the slices of logs.

▶ Show the children how they can line up several log slices and link them with 'bridges' made from the thin flat softwood off-cuts.

▶ Drill any extra holes that the children need into any of the resources.

Key vocabulary and questions

▶ hold, still, position, steady, cover, space, amount, half, section

▶ pattern, design

Safety issues

▶ Show children how to safely and correctly hammer in the nails and the other items – repeat the instructions several times.

▶ Ensure children are not too close to each other to work safely.

▶ Show the correct storage of hammers and remaining nails after use.

Making a log creature

What you need:

- a softwood log (approx. 400-500mm long)
- hammers and nails in various sizes
- brown sugar paper, black felt-tipped pen, thick string
- cardboard pre-cut into triangular and rectangular pieces
- carpet off-cuts/squares
- scissors
- rulers
- mini awl (for adult use)
- bubble wrap, corrugated card, food packaging

What you do:

- Provide the resources and tools for children to use, including the pre-cut cardboard triangles and rectangles.
- Cover the table with the carpet off-cuts and place the log on top, tying it on to the table with thick string to prevent it from wobbling.
- Tell the children that you are going to nail pieces of paper and cardboard onto the log and turn the log into a fantastic creature!

- ▶ Encourage the children to glue bubble wrap, corrugated card, food packaging, etc. onto the cardboard triangles, before nailing them on to the log, to create a 'spiky, lumpy, bumpy creature'.

- ▶ Children, in turn, choose a cardboard triangle and nail it onto the log. Help each child as necessary, e.g. by holding the piece of cardboard in place as they nail it.

- ▶ Ask a child to draw a 'face' on the sugar paper, cut round it if necessary, and nail it in place.

- ▶ Ask another child to nail the cardboard 'legs' onto the log – you may want to cut these into leg/feet shapes.

- ▶ Collect logs of different shapes, and ask children what they remind them of so children can transform them into their own unique 'creatures'.

- ▶ Make a crocodile by painting the log green and nailing on cardboard 'jaws', and 'teeth' (paper cut with pinking shears). Or you could make a scaly fish based on children's ideas!

Key vocabulary and questions

- ▶ curved, slanting, sloping, pointing, direction, position, edge, underneath, on top, at the side
- ▶ Where will your spike go?
- ▶ Where will you put the nail?

Safety issues

- ▶ Show children how to safely and correctly use the hammer. Model its use and give guidance several times.

- ▶ Ensure children are not too close to each other to work safely.

- ▶ Show children the correct storage of tools after use.

- ▶ For some children it may be necessary, when they have said where they want the nail to go, for the adult to use a mini awl to make a hole through the cardboard and into the log, to get the children started.

Making a basic model car

What you need:

▶ child-sized hammers
▶ 2 pre-cut pieces of planed softwood timber for each child:
  (one piece of wood larger than the other)
▶ plastic screw on tops from milk cartons with an 4mm hole
  pre-drilled (by an adult)
▶ roundhead nails 25mm long
▶ awl (for adult use only)
▶ PVA glue and spreaders
▶ masking tape, chunky woodworking pencil, felt tipped pens, sanding block

N.B. If the children want to paint the car later then provide paint with PVA glue
added and suitably sized brushes.

What you do:

▶ Provide the required resources and tools for each child to
  access.

▶ Model and then encourage the children to sand the two pre-cut
  pieces of softwood.

- ▶ Explain to the children that you are going to make a model car.

- ▶ Demonstrate gluing the two pieces of wood together and then fastening them together using masking tape. The smaller piece of wood should be fixed on top of the larger piece. (This will avoid having to wait for the glue to dry and allow the children to get on with making the car!)

- ▶ Pre-mark four holes using a pencil and then use an awl to make small indentation/starter holes, into the side of the larger piece of wood, ready to nail on the wheels. (This is an adult only part of the activity with children watching.)

- ▶ Explain the correct and safe use of the hammer and nails. Demonstrate hammering the head of a nail to drive it into the side of the wood through the screw top. (The screw tops will make the wheels of the car.)

- ▶ Allow the children to hammer in the nails, encouraging them to concentrate and not to rush!

- ▶ Encourage the children to draw the doors, windows, windscreen and the number plate onto the car using the woodworking pencil or felt tip pens.

- ▶ Remind the children to replace the tools when the activity is finished.

Key vocabulary and questions

- ▶ wheels, hole, windscreen, number plate, rotate, windows
- ▶ Can you hammer the wheels onto the car?
- ▶ Can you rotate/turn the wheels after you hammer them onto the car?

Safety issues

- ▶ Show children how to safely and correctly hammer the nail through the plastic screw tops (the wheels) into the side of the wood (the car) and give guidance several times and then support independent use.

- ▶ Ensure children are not too close to each other.

- ▶ Remind the children about the correct storage of hammer, nails, glue and pencil afterwards.

Making a basic model helicopter

What you need:

- ▶ child-sized hammers
- ▶ 2 ready cut pieces of planed softwood timber (one three times larger than the other) for each child:
  (i) approx. 100mm x 50mm x 150mm;
  (ii) approx. 100mm x 50mm x 50mm
- ▶ 2 plastic lolly sticks (for helicopter blades) with a 4mm hole pre-drilled in the centre for each child
- ▶ nails (15mm long) with a smaller diameter than the pre-drilled hole in the lolly sticks
- ▶ awl (for adult use)
- ▶ glue and spreaders, masking tape, chunky woodworking pencil, sanding block

What you do:

▶ Explain to the children that you are going to make a model helicopter.

▶ Provide the resources and tools for children to access.

▶ Ask the children to sand the two pre-cut pieces of softwood.

▶ Demonstrate gluing the two pieces together to create the basic form of the helicopter and then fastening using masking tape. (This will avoid waiting for the glue to dry, allowing the children to get on with making the rest of the helicopter!)

▶ Pre-mark the hole for nailing the helicopter blades on using a pencil, then an awl to make a small indentation/starter hole for hammering (adult with children watching).

▶ Help the children to hammer the head of the nail through the centre of two lolly sticks into the wood to form the blades.

▶ Encouage the children to draw the windows of the helicopter and write its code on the sides using the pencil.

Key vocabulary and questions

▶ wheels, hole, helicopter windscreen, blades, rotate, windows

▶ Can you nail the blades onto the top of the helicopter?

▶ Can you rotate/turn the blades after you hammer them on?

Safety issues

▶ Show children how to safely and correctly hammer the nail through the hole in the plastic blades – give guidance several times.

▶ Ensure children are not too close to each other when hammering.

▶ Remind children about the correct storage of hammer, nails, glue and pencil afterwards.

Making a basic model aeroplane

What you need:

▶ hammers and roundhead nails 10mm long

▶ one ready cut and shaped piece of planed softwood timber
(for the form of the aeroplane) approx. 100mm x 40mm x 250mm long

▶ scissors and cardboard (to cut out the wing and tailfin)

▶ glue and spreaders, chunky woodworking pencil, sanding block

What you do:

▶ Provide the resources and tools for children to access.

▶ Explain and demonstrate the activity for the children. Tell them that they are going to make a model aeroplane.

▶ Encourage the children to sand the pre-cut shaped piece of softwood for the body (fuselage) of the aeroplane.

▶ Help the children to cut out the wings and two pieces of tail fin from the cardboard. Glue the wings in place.

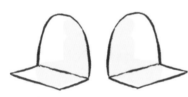

▶ Support the children in hammering the nails to doubly secure the already glued on wings to the body of the plane.

▶ Help the children to make and glue on the tail fin.

▶ Model and encourage the children to decorate the plane by drawing in windows and adding wing symbols and numbers using a chunky woodworking pencil.

▶ As a possible extension activity, investigate with the children what kinds of imaginary birds or flying reptiles you could create using the above basic design for an aeroplane as a starting point.

Key vocabulary and questions

▶ aeroplane, flying, sky, fuselage, wings, tail
▶ What are the wings on an aeroplane for?
▶ Will your aeroplane fly?

Safety issues

▶ Show children how to safely and correctly hammer the nails, giving guidance several times if required.

▶ Ensure children are not too close to each other when hammering so they can work safely.

▶ Remind the children about the correct storage of hammer, nails, scissors, glue and pencil afterwards.

(B) Emerging skills level

Tools and other resources required for this level

All those from the 'Beginner level' plus:

▶ a mini hand-drill

▶ drill bits 4, 5, and 6mm diameter

▶ wooden dowling (6mm diameter)

▶ woodwork bench with vice* (*for adult guided use)

▶ 150mm flat measuring rule

▶ larger variety of nails, both flat and round heads between 12mm-60mm

ALL TOOLS SHOULD BE STORED IN A SAFE BUT ACCESSIBLE WAY E.G. USING SILHOUTTES ON SHELVES OR ON A RACK.

Drilling into a cardboard shoe box

What you need:

► a mini hand-drill

► drill bits (6mm)

► a shoe box packed tightly with layered cardboard (cut from supermarket type boxes) with ready drilled starter holes in the top of the box lid

► masking tape

N.B. This is an ideal activity for outdoors.

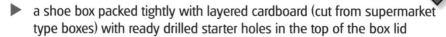

What you do:

▶ Provide the resources and tools for children to access.

▶ Show the children the mini hand-drill and bits, and explain their purpose.

▶ Carefully show them the drill and then show them how to use it safely.

▶ Let the children roll a drill bit on a flat surface, and notice how the pattern in the metal appears to 'move downwards'.

▶ Show them how the bit is fitted tightly into the hand-drill.

▶ Demonstrate how the drill works and let each child have a turn – moving it very slowly.

▶ Show the children the layered cardboard inside the shoe box (ensure that it is tightly packed in), then tape the shoe box shut.

▶ Demonstrate the use of the drill to make holes. Show the children how different sizes of holes are made with the different sized bits.

▶ Supervise each child to experiment freely with the drill to make different sized holes in the shoe box. Adults can change the bits periodically.

Key vocabulary and questions

▶ drill, drill bit, drilling, rotate, bores in, hole, sharp

▶ Why does the drill bit make a hole?

▶ Can you see the bit rotating and drilling into the box?

▶ How does it feel as the drill bores in?

Safety issues

▶ Show the children how to safely and correctly use the drill and drill bit, repeating the guidance several times.

▶ Ensure children are not too close to each other when drilling.

▶ Show children the correct and safe storage of the drill and drill bits.

Drilling holes in a piece of softwood

What you need:

- a mini hand-drill
- drill bits (4, 5 and 6mm)
- woodwork bench with vice (to hold piece of wood)
- large piece of softwood fastened securely in the vice
- awl (optional, for adult use only to start holes prior to drilling)

What you do:

▶ Provide the resources and tools for children to access.

▶ Show them how to secure the wood in the vice.

▶ Demonstrate how to use the mini hand-drill and bits, and explain their purpose.

▶ Demonstrate how the drill works and let each child have a turn, moving it very slowly.

▶ Show the children how different sizes of holes are made with the different drill bits.

▶ Allow each child in turn to freely use the drill to make holes in the wood.

▶ The adult can pre-drill/start off holes for the children using an awl.

Key vocabulary and questions

▶ drilling, bit turning, hole, different sizes

▶ How does the drill bit make a hole?

▶ What is happening as you make the hole?

Safety issues

▶ Show children how to safely and correctly use the drill and drill bit, giving guidance several times as required.

▶ Ensure children are not too close to each other when drilling.

▶ Show children the correct storage of the drill and drill bits.

Making a name plaque

What you need:

▶ a mini hand-drill with 6mm drill bit

▶ woodwork bench with vice

▶ suitable piece of softwood or plywood (e.g. 100mm x 150mm x 6mm thick)

▶ sand paper block, woodworking pencil, measuring rule, felt-tip pens (range of colours), watered down PVA glue (one part glue to one part water) and brushes

What you do:

▶ Provide the resources and tools for children to access.

▶ Explain to the children they will be making and decorating a name plaque and show them a finished name plaque (if you have one).

▶ Ask the children to sandpaper the piece of wood until smooth on both the surfaces and the edges.

▶ Support the children in marking two holes in the centre top of the longer side of the wood – 25mm in from the edge (use the measuring rule). These holes are for hanging the name plaques up.

▶ Make a 'pilot' hole on the markings using an awl (adult with children watching).

▶ Secure the wood in the vice, with the side that will be the front of the plaque facing to the front, and help a child to drill one of the holes.

▶ Loosen the vice and turn the wood around and secure again in the vice (with the side that will be the front of the plaque facing the front) then help a child to drill the second hole.

▶ Ask the children to sand over any rough parts which have appeared as a result of the drilling.

▶ Encourage the children to carefully write their name in large letters in pencil or felt-tip pens on one flat face of the wooden piece, then decorate as they wish.

▶ Once finished, ask the children to paint their name plaque with one light coat of diluted PVA glue. This will dry clear and seal in their artwork.

Key vocabulary and questions

▶ rough, smooth, front face, tighten, loosen, diluted, pilot hole

▶ How long is 25mm on the ruler?

▶ What happened when the diluted PVA glue dried?

Safety issues

▶ Show children how to safely and correctly use the drill and drill bit, giving guidance several times as required.

▶ Ensure children are not too close to each other when drilling.

▶ Remind children about the correct storage of the drill and drill bits.

Making a basic model aeroplane with propellers

What you need:

- ▶ picture of a model propeller powered aeroplane (from internet or magazine)
- ▶ suitably sized pre-cut piece of soft wood for the body of the aeroplane (the fuselage) approx. 100mm x 50mm x 300mm
- ▶ hammers and round head nails (10mm long)
- ▶ one ready cut and shaped piece of planed softwood timber (for the wings) approx. 100mm x 12mm x 200mm long
- ▶ hand-drill with 4mm drill bit
- ▶ thick cardboard (to cut out tail fin and propellers)
- ▶ PVA glue and spreaders, chunky woodworking pencil, sanding block, scissors, masking tape and felt-tipped pens
- ▶ two plastic bottle tops

What you do:

- ▶ Provide the resources and tools for children to access.
- ▶ Show the children the parts of the model aeroplane, noticing its fuselage, wings, propellers and tail fin.
- ▶ Sand the wooden pieces.

- ▶ Draw two tail fin shapes on cardboard, providing any necessary help.
- ▶ Ask the children to cut out each shape of the tail fin, fold it in the middle and glue the two pieces together.

- ▶ Then ask them to stick the folded tail fin, with a small piece of folded masking tape, on top of the very end of the piece of wood, to keep it in position temporarily as they will later need to nail the tail fin onto the wood, using a nail on each side.
- ▶ Mark two spots at the front of the timber wing piece on each side.
- ▶ Then nail two small pre-drilled plastic bottle tops to the front of the wing piece, leaving enough space so these still rotate.
- ▶ Glue the wing piece across the top of the fuselage and then secure further using two nails.
- ▶ Ask the children to cut out two strips of cardboard for each propeller.
- ▶ Help the children to glue the propellers onto the front of the bottle tops attached to the wings.
- ▶ Using a felt-tipped pen, children can decorate the wings and tail fin, and draw porthole windows and doors on the fuselage.

Key vocabulary and questions

- ▶ fuselage, length, width, across, front, back, rotate, propellers
- ▶ Are the wings longer or shorter than the length of the fuselage?
- ▶ Can you rotate the propellers on your model?
- ▶ What is the shape of the tail fin?

Safety issues

- ▶ Show children how to safely and correctly hammer the nails.
- ▶ Ensure children are not too close to each other.
- ▶ Show children the correct storage of tools and nails after use.

Making a basic sailing boat

What you need:

▶ picture of a toy/model sailing boat

▶ ready cut piece of planed softwood timber approx. 100mm x 75mm x 300mm long with 45° pointed end (to make a basic boat shape)

▶ scrap material to cut out a sail, scissors

▶ hand-drill and 6mm drill bit

▶ chunky woodworking pencil, sanding block, PVA glue and spreaders, felt-tip pens

▶ piece of 6mm (diameter) dowelling cut to 150mm in length

▶ saw to shape wood (adult use only)

What you do:

▶ Look at the parts of the toy/model boat, noticing its sail.

▶ Provide the resources and tools for children to access.

▶ Sand the cut boat shape until it is smooth all over.

▶ Mark a central point in the top of the boat for the sail.

▶ Make a pilot hole using an awl (adult with children watching).

▶ Drill a hole into the boat where marked to fit the sail mast.

▶ Take the cut 6mm diameter dowelling piece and sandpaper lightly around the bottom part to make it fit into the drilled hole.

▶ Add glue to the bottom edge of the dowelling once it fits into the hole and glue in place.

▶ Cut two sail-shaped pieces out of scrap material, paper or thin card.

▶ Show the children the sail shapes (triangular template) and ask them to draw round them and then cut them out from a piece of material. You should have two pieces approximately the same size.

▶ Encourage the children to decorate the sails with the felt-tip pens.

▶ Glue the sails onto the mast so that the two pieces are one each side and the two faces of the sail are stuck together on each side of the 'mast'.

Key vocabulary and questions

▶ width, diameter, triangle shape, depth, sailing, sail, mast, pilot hole

▶ How did you know not to drill too deep for the sail mast?

▶ How is a sailing boat powered?

Safety issues

▶ Remind the children how to safely and correctly use the drill.

▶ Ensure children are not too close to each other.

▶ Show the correct storage of tools after the activity is finished.

Making a mini sculpture

What you need:

▶ variety of wood off-cuts, some straight and some curved

▶ child-sized hammer and variety of nails

▶ glue and spreader, sandpaper blocks

▶ a piece of softwood approx. 100mm x 100mm x 20mm (for the base), a piece 30mm x 30mm x 200mm long (to be inserted into the base)

▶ small, thin off-cuts

▶ plastic screw on milk bottle tops of different colours with a predrilled hole in the centre

▶ corrugated card off-cuts from boxes (stiff type) and scrap materials

▶ woodwork bench and vice

What you do:

▶ Show the children a pre-made wooden model sculpture (if possible) and explain how they are going to make a sculpture by nailing things into pieces of wood but that it will be unique and different from the one you have shown them.

▶ Talk about their ideas with them.

▶ Demonstrate that the 30mm x 30mm x 200mm piece of wood will be upright and fastened to the base to make a stand. Explain that they will nail items onto the basic sculpture.

▶ Show them that they can use the drill to create hole patterns in the off-cuts and encourage them to try this.

▶ Show the children how they can use the card off-cuts to create interesting shapes and nail these on.

▶ Encourage the children to sand the pieces, particularly around the edges, until they are smooth.

▶ Explain how they can glue and nail pieces together so they won't fall apart later.

▶ Help them to fasten their sculpture to the base of the stand.

▶ Provide individual support as needed.

Key vocabulary and questions

▶ sculpture, shapes, curved, straight, upright, unique
▶ What pattern will you make using the drill?
▶ How can we get these pieces to join together?

Safety issues

▶ Remind the children how to safely and correctly use the hammer, nails and drill.

▶ Ensure children are not too close to each other.

▶ Show the correct storage of tools after the activity.

Making a giant outdoor sculpture

What you need:

- ▶ a large piece of timber nailed securely to a fence in your outdoor area
- ▶ large variety of shapes/sizes of wood
- ▶ child-sized hammers and variety of small nails
- ▶ workbench and vice

What you do:

- ▶ Explain to the children you are going to make a large outdoor sculpture.

- ▶ Explain that this sculpture is going to be a group one and is going to be outdoors! Talk about safety and that the rule is only one person at a time can add to the sculpture.

- ▶ Talk about their ideas with them.

- ▶ Take them outdoors and show them the large timber piece that is secured to a fence.

- ▶ Demonstrate how they can use the drill to create hole patterns in the wood and encourage them to try this.

- ▶ Demonstrate how they can glue and nail pieces together so they won't fall apart later!

- ▶ Provide ongoing support and advice as needed.

- ▶ Take some photographs of the children with the finished sculpture!

Key vocabulary and questions

- ▶ sculpture, shapes, curved, straight, upright
- ▶ What pattern will you make using the drill?
- ▶ How can we get these pieces to join together?

Safety issues

- ▶ Remind the children how to safely and correctly use the hammer, nails and drill.
- ▶ Ensure children are not too close to each other.
- ▶ Show the correct storage of tools after the activity is finished.

Making a simple model steam train

What you need (for each child):

I will need

▶ hammers and roundhead nails (12mm long)

▶ one ready cut and shaped piece of planed softwood timber approx. 150mm x 50mm x 300mm long (for the main body of the train)

▶ one ready cut and shaped piece of planed softwood timber approx. 150mm x 150mm x 100mm (for the engine cab)

▶ one pre-cut piece of planed softwood dowelling approx. 25mm diameter x 40mm long (for the funnel)

▶ glue and spreaders, chunky woodworking pencil, sanding block

▶ six small plastic bottle tops pre-drilled (for train wheels)

▶ mini hand-drill

▶ awl (for adult use only)

What you do:

▶ Provide the resources and tools for children to access.

▶ At each stage of making the model train, explain and model what you are doing for the children.

▶ Encourage the children to sand the pre-cut piece of softwood.

▶ Pre-mark holes along both sides of the train (for the 6 wheels) using a pencil, then an awl to make a small indentation/starter hole (with children watching). The wood is now ready for children to hammer a nail into a bottle top to make a wheel.

▶ Support children nailing the wheels on so that they rotate. Ensure the correct and safe use of the hammer and nails at all times.

▶ Model gluing the circular dowel pieces to the top of the train, explaining this is the chimney (or funnel) for the steam to come out.

▶ Encourage the children to concentrate and not to rush!

▶ Ask the children to decorate the train using the pencil once the glue has dried. They can draw in the windows, any identification letters/numbers and any other features they would like to add!

Key vocabulary and questions

▶ train, steam, engine, driver, track, windows, funnel, cab

▶ What is the funnel/chimney on top of the train for?

▶ What do trains travel on?

Safety issues

▶ As always, show children how to safely and correctly hammer the nails, demonstrate several times if required.

▶ Ensure children are not too close to each other when hammering e.g. a left-handed child should not be next to a right-handed child.

▶ Remind children about the correct storage of hammer, nails, glue and pencil afterwards.

What can I make?

Assessment activity

This activity should take place only after children have experienced a wide range of activities and developed their skills in using tools effectively and safely. This activity is for you to assess whether the children need more experience at this level or are ready to move onto the next level.

What you need:

A range of resources and tools that you have used in previous activities from:

- ▶ different sizes and shapes of wood off-cuts
- ▶ child-sized hammers and nails
- ▶ mini hand-drill and drill bits
- ▶ cardboard
- ▶ glue, scissors, woodworking pencils and felt-tip pens
- ▶ screw tops and material fabric
- ▶ sanding blocks
- ▶ any other suitable items that children suggest

What you do:

- ▶ Ask the children to remind you what they have made in previous activities. What did they enjoy the most? Did they find anything hard to do? Ask them to think what they would like to make. Explore their ideas with them.

- ▶ Encourage the children to choose from the range of resources and tools provided to make their choice, this might be something made in a previous activity or something new e.g. a bird table or a bus.

- ▶ Give them the support and advice they ask for/need.

- ▶ Take photographs of the process and the final results!

Key vocabulary and questions

- ▶ words relevant to the task
- ▶ How can you join these?
- ▶ How can you do it safely?

Safety issues

- ▶ Remind children how to safely and correctly handle the tools, provide guidance and support as required.
- ▶ Ensure children are not too close to each other when hammering or drilling.
- ▶ Remind children about the correct storage of tools and equipment after they have finished the activity.

(C) Developing competence level

Tools and other resources required for this level

Those for Beginner and Emerging levels plus:

- ▶ 8mm and 10mm wood bits
- ▶ carpenter's square
- ▶ claw hammer
- ▶ loose sandpaper, (semi-rough and fine)
- ▶ wooden sanding block
- ▶ screw driver (cross head)
- ▶ screws (cross head and slot head)
- ▶ chunky pliers (to extract nails)
- ▶ mini awl
- ▶ mini tenon saw
- ▶ retractable measuring tape
- ▶ mini spirit level

ALL TOOLS SHOULD BE STORED IN A SAFE BUT ACCESSIBLE WAY E.G. USING SILHOUTTES ON SHELVES OR ON A RACK. N.B. PARTICULAR ATTENTION MUST BE GIVEN TO THE STORAGE OF SAWS.

Screwing into softwood

What you need:

▶ woodwork bench with vice

▶ large piece of softwood

▶ screwdrivers

▶ crosshead wood screws (8mm long)

▶ mini awl (adult use only)

▶ woodworking pencil

What you do:

▶ In small groups of 3-6 children provide the resources and tools for children to access.

▶ Model the safe and correct use of a screwdriver to screw a nail into the piece of wood.

▶ Ask the children to mark a point on the wood then drill a pilot hole.

▶ Then help them to use a screwdriver to fix a screw into the wood.

▶ Challenge the children to see if they can now unscrew the nails!

Key vocabulary and questions

▶ screwdriver, crosshead, screws, pilot hole

▶ Is it hard to fix a screw?

▶ What is the most difficult thing you have got to learn to do this?

Safety issues

▶ Ensure that you model the use of the screws and screwdriver, several times if neccessary.

▶ Encourage the children to concentrate and take their time!

Making a coat hook

What you need:

- ▶ woodwork bench with vice
- ▶ pre-cut piece of planed softwood (100mm x 100mm x 20mm)
- ▶ cup hooks
- ▶ hand-drill and 6mm drill bit
- ▶ sanding block, woodworking pencil
- ▶ mini awl

What you do:

▶ Provide the resources and tools for children to access.

▶ Explain to the children that they will make a coat hook.

▶ Ask the children to sand the wood until smooth.

▶ Mark a hole 20mm from the top edge and then the bottom edge of the wood.

▶ Place the wood in the vice and make pilot holes using the awl (adult use only).

▶ Support the children in drilling the two marked holes using the 6mm wood drill bit – drill right through. These are for fixing the hook to a wall or door.

▶ Ask the children to sandpaper any roughness caused by the drilling.

▶ Place the hook on the surface of the wood where it is to be sited and mark the holes onto the wood.

▶ Use an awl to make a pilot hole (adult use only).

▶ Help the children to screw the hook into the cut wood.

▶ As an extension activity ask the children to suggest how to make a coat hook that will hold more than one coat!

Key vocabulary and questions

▶ pilot hole, coat hook
▶ Is it hard to fix a screw?
▶ Where would you like to fix this at home?

Safety issues

▶ Ensure that you model the use of the screws and screwdriver, several times if neccessary.

▶ Encourage the children to concentrate and take their time!

Nailing then extracting using a claw hammer

What you need:

- a block of softwood
- claw hammer
- variety of nails (but none above 40mm long)
- woodwork bench with vice
- safety goggles (for each child)

What you do:

▶ Provide the resources and tools for children to access.

▶ Demonstrate how to safely nail and then extract nails from the piece of softwood using a claw hammer.

▶ Provide the large piece of planed softwood for children to hammer nails into (which needs to be fixed securely into the vice).

▶ Ask the children to only partly hammer the nails into the wood. Then allow them to attempt to pull these out using a claw hammer.

Key vocabulary and questions

▶ claw hammer, extract, partly

▶ How is it best to use the claw to pull out nails?

▶ What advice could you give others when trying to extract nails?

Safety issues

▶ Children must be shown how to secure each nail in the claw and then how to pull out each nail steadily and carefully.

▶ Children must wear safety goggles for this activity.

▶ Be careful to ensure that children dispose of the nails in the bin carefully when they have been extracted.

▶ Ensure that children have plenty of space and are not too close together when using a claw hammer to extract nails.

Sawing into wood

What you need:

- ▶ pieces of softwood
- ▶ mini tenon saw
- ▶ woodwork bench with vice
- ▶ carpenter's square and woodworking pencil
- ▶ safety goggles and protective gloves

I will need

What you do:

▶ With one child at a time, provide the resources and tools for the child to access.

▶ The child selects a piece of wood and secures it in the vice (with your support).

▶ The adult models use of the mini tenon saw to cut the wood.

▶ Use the carpenter's square and a pencil to mark a line on the wood and cut along this line.

▶ Carefully supervise the child in using the tenon saw to cut into the wood.

Key vocabulary and questions

▶ tenon saw, cut, teeth, safety block guard, vice, tighten, sawdust, carpenters square, left handed, right handed

▶ What happens to the wood as you use the saw to cut?

▶ Are you left handed or right handed?

Safety issues

▶ Be careful to ensure that children think about safety when handling or using saws and understand why this is important!

▶ Show them how sharp the teeth of a saw are.

▶ Ensure the children check that the wood is securely fixed in the vice before cutting.

▶ Keep the area clean and as dust free as possible by regularly brushing up sawdust and any off-cuts on the floor.

▶ Ensure children wear safety goggles and a protective glove when sawing.

▶ Ensure children take extra care when putting away saws after use.

Nailing then extracting using pliers

What you need:

▶ block of planed softwood

▶ chunky pliers

▶ variety of nails (none above 25mm in length)

▶ woodwork bench with vice

▶ safety goggles

What you do:

▶ Provide the resources and tools for children to access.

▶ Ensure that the large piece of planed softwood is fixed securely into the vice.

▶ Support the children in hammering nails into the wood.

▶ Demonstrate how to safely extract a nail using the pliers.

▶ Ask the children to only partly hammer the nails into the wood. Then allow them to attempt to pull these out using chunky pliers.

Key vocabulary and questions

▶ pliers, chunky, thin, extract, partly

▶ What is the best way to use the pliers to pull out nails?

▶ What advice could you give others when using pliers to extract nails?

Safety issues

▶ Ensure that children dispose of the nails in the bin carefully when these have been extracted.

▶ Make sure the children have plenty of space and are not too close together when using pliers to extract nails.

▶ Safety goggles must be worn when extracting nails.

Making a small world tree

What you need:

▶ mini hand-drill and drill bits (4, 5 and 6mm)

▶ flat off-cut of approx. 60mm x 60mm x 20mm thick piece of softwood (for the base)

▶ sanding block

▶ mini tenon saw

▶ twigs and torn pieces of green tissue paper or thin card

▶ PVA glue in a squeezy container, glue spreader, plasticine

▶ scissors and pencil

▶ safety goggles

What you do:

▶ With an appropriately-sized small group of children, provide the resources and tools for children to access.

▶ Explain that you are going to make a tree for your small world play area. Model the entire activity for the children's understanding.

▶ Ask the children to sand the pieces of softwood.

▶ Encourage the children to look at the width of the twigs and support one child at a time to use a mini tenon saw to cut a twig to a smaller size/length as required. Ensure twigs are fastened securely in the vice.

▶ Encourage the children to look at the diameter of the twig and decide which size of bit to use to drill a hole.

▶ Support a child to drill one hole in the centre of the base, taking care not to drill right through the wood.

▶ Sandpaper down the bottom diameter of the twig if it is slightly too big for the hole.

▶ Children carefully glue the twig into the hole and allow to dry.

▶ Draw and cut out the card leaves, decorate and then glue these to the top parts of the twig once the glue has dried at the joint. You could also glue torn pieces of green tissue paper on as leaves.

▶ Use plasticine to pack round the base of the 'tree' to ensure the joint is more stable.

▶ As an extension activity ask children to suggest how they could make a row or 'hedge' of trees.

Key vocabulary and questions

▶ smooth, edges, neater, finish, size, length, straight, crooked, join

▶ How do you know how deep to drill the hole?

▶ What would happen if you drilled too deeply?

▶ How do you know when to stop drilling?

Safety issues

▶ Show children how to safely and correctly use the drill – give instruction several times as necessary.

▶ Ensure children are not too close to each other.

▶ Show correct storage of drill after use.

▶ Ensure children wear safety goggles when sawing wood.

What can I make?

Assessment activity

This activity should take place only after children have experienced a wide range of activities and developed skills in using tools effectively and safely. This activity is ideal for you to assess whether the children need more experience at this level or are ready to move on to the next level.

What you need:

▶ a range of resources and tools that you have used in previous activities: mini tenon saws, pliers and nails, screw driver and screws, wood off-cuts, hammer, scissors, glue spreaders, pencils, tissue paper and card.

What you do:

▶ Ask the children to remind you what they have made in previous activities. What did they enjoy the most? Did they find anything hard to do? Ask them to think what they would like to make. Explore their ideas with them.

▶ Encourage the children to choose from the range of resources and tools you have provided as much to make their choice.

▶ Give them as much support and advice as they ask for/need.

Key vocabulary and questions

▶ words relevant to the task

▶ How can you join these?

▶ How can you do it safely?

Safety issues

▶ Remind children how to safely and correctly handle the tools, give guidance several times if required.

▶ Ensure children are not too close to each other when hammering.

▶ Ensure children are wearing safety goggles.

▶ Remind children about the correct storage of equipment after they have finished the activity.

D) Advanced competence level

Tools and other resources required for this level

Those for Beginner, Emerging and Developing competence levels plus:

- standard screws – single slotted head
- standard screw drivers – single slotted head
- mini hacksaw
- wide wood bits for the hand held drill
- g-clamps

**ALL TOOLS SHOULD BE STORED IN A SAFE BUT ACCESSIBLE WAY
E.G. USING SILHOUTTES ON SHELVES OR ON A RACK.
(N.B. PARTICULAR ATTENTION MUST BE GIVEN TO THE STORAGE OF SAWS)**

Making a coaster

What you need:

- square flat off-cuts approx. 100mm x 100mm x 6mm
- sanding blocks
- mini hand-drill and 4mm drill bit
- paper and pencils
- set square
- g-clamp or vice

What you do:

- Ask the children to smooth the off-cuts with sanding blocks.
- Explain and demonstrate to the children that they can decorate their coaster by making a pattern of shallow holes with the smallest-sized bit (4mm) e.g. in the centre and/or round the edge as a border. Use the set square to give you 90° corners in your patterns.
- Children can use paper and pencil to draw their planned pattern of holes.
- Children can use the hand-drill to make their pattern on their coaster – ensure the wood is securely fastened to the bench using a g-clamp or vice.

Key vocabulary and questions

- shallow, deep, middle, centre, edge, border
- What would happen to the holes if you did not hold your drill straight upwards?

Safety issues

- Show children how to safely and correctly use the drill. Model and give guidance several times.
- Ensure children are not too close to each other
- Show the correct storage of tools after the activity is finished.

Making a teapot stand

What you need:

▶ 1 flat piece of softwood off-cut (approx. 150mm x 150mm x 12mm deep)

▶ short pieces of 10mm dowelling for the child to cut to size

▶ sanding blocks

▶ mini hand-drill and 10mm drill bit

▶ paper, pencils, felt-tip pens, PVA glue

▶ mini hacksaw

▶ safety goggles

What you do:

▶ Ask the children to smooth the softwood piece for the stand with sanding blocks until smooth.

▶ Mark and then drill four holes approx. 10mm deep on each corner of the off-cut – approx. 25mm in from the edges using 10mm wood drill bit.

▶ Using the hacksaw, cut the 10mm diameter dowels into four pieces at 25mm long.

▶ Sandpaper the bottom edges of the cut dowel pieces so these will fit into the drilled holes.

▶ Glue the cut dowels into the holes using PVA glue and leave to dry.

▶ Children can decorate their teapot stands with simple patterns using felt tip pens and pencils.

▶ Paint on watered down PVA glue to seal the stand.

Key vocabulary and questions

▶ shallow, deep, middle, centre, edge, border

▶ What would happen to the holes if you did not hold your drill straight upwards?

Safety issues

▶ Show children how to safely and correctly use the drill. Model and give guidance several times.

▶ Ensure children are not too close to each other.

▶ Show the correct storage of tools after use.

▶ Ensure children are wearing safety goggles when sawing.

Making a letter rack

What you need:

▶ softwood off-cut approx. 150mm x 60mm x 6mm deep

▶ sanding block

▶ hand drill and drill bits (6mm)

▶ a length of dowelling (300mm long)

▶ measuring rule, woodworking pencil, PVA glue, glue spreaders

▶ mini hacksaw (to cut dowelling to size)

▶ vice

What you do:

▶ Children sand the large off-cut for the base of the rack.

▶ Help the children to cut the dowel into four pieces of 75mm, making sure it is securely fastened in the vice.

▶ The children then sand the ends of the four pieces of newly cut dowel.

▶ Mark four crosses in the corners of the base about 25mm in from each edge to show the children where the holes for the dowel pieces should go.

▶ Ask the children to look at the diameter of the dowel and decide which size of drill bit to use.

▶ Help the children to drill four holes where the marks are, taking care not to drill through the off-cut base.

▶ Children should push each of the dowel pieces into the holes, using a little glue on the end if necessary.

▶ Allow to dry.

▶ The letter rack is now ready for letters to be slotted into at an angle.

▶ As a follow up from this activity, ask the children to think how to adapt this letter rack design into something else, e.g. a tea-towel holder (wall-mounted)? Could they make a simple 'mug tree' to hold two mugs?

Key vocabulary and questions

▶ How wide, width, will it fit, wide enough, how deep, depth, too deep, top right hand corner, centimetre, position, bottom left hand corner, dowel, diagonally, slanting

▶ How do we know which sized drill bit to use?

▶ How do we know when to stop drilling?

▶ What will happen if we drill too deeply?

Safety issues

▶ Show children how to safely and correctly use the drill. Model and give guidance several times.

▶ Ensure children are not too close to each other.

▶ Show the correct storage of tools after use.

Making a dolls' house chair

What you need:

▶ rectangular-shaped softwood off-cut approx. 150mm x 50mm x 12mm deep for the back of the chair

▶ a block-shaped softwood off-cut approx. 50mm x 50mm x 50mm deep for the seat of the chair

▶ sanding block

▶ masking tape

▶ hammer, 4 nails (approx. 20mm deep)

What you do:

▶ Children sand the two off-cuts, as much as required.

▶ Then help them to place the rectangular-shaped off-cut at right angles to the block, to make a chair shape and fix them temporarily in place with small pieces of folded parcel tape.

▶ Allow the children to decide on the best position to place the chair on the work surface as they nail the 'back' of the chair to the 'seat' – using four nails.

▶ As a follow up to the activity ask the children to think of any other ways to make a dolls' house chair? Or other dolls' house furniture?

Key vocabulary and questions

▶ rectangular back, seat, temporarily, position, corners, side, upright, join, upside down, back, front

▶ Where do you think you should hammer the nails to join the back of the chair to the seat?

Safety issues

▶ Adult to use a mini awl to start off the nail holes for the children – modelling its safe use.

▶ Ensure children are not too close to each other.

▶ Remind children of the correct storage of tools after use.

Making a bead necklace

What you need:

- ▶ small elderberry branches minimum 8mm thick (the thicker the better) and approx. 300mm long

- ▶ metal meat skewer (for adult use only)

- ▶ thin nylon fishing line

- ▶ mini hack saw

- ▶ woodwork bench and vice

- ▶ berries (to make colouring) or food colouring

What you do:

▶ Show the children a ready cut piece of elderberry branch.

▶ Explain how you are going to use the meat skewer to push out the soft centre of the branch and then cut it into cylindrical beads.

▶ Then, while the children are watching, clear the soft centre using the meat skewer.

▶ Provide a range of branches cut to size with the centres already cleared out for the children to use.

▶ Secure the branch in the vice and then demonstrate cutting the beads using the mini hacksaw. These can be cut to various lengths.

▶ Help the children to cut their own branches into cylindrical beads.

▶ When the beads are cut, dip them into a shallow bowl of food colouring. Leave them to soak for 5 minutes and then lay them on a tissue to dry.

▶ Once the beads are dry, thread them onto nylon fishing lines to make necklaces.

Key vocabulary and questions

▶ elderberry, meat skewer, bead necklace, thread

▶ How can you thread the beads onto the line?

▶ Is it easier or harder to thread smaller beads/bigger beads?

Safety issues

▶ Ensure branch is securely held in vice.

▶ Encourage the children to concentrate and not to rush but to take their time.

▶ Demonstrate the correct storage of tools after use.

▶ Ensure children are wearing goggles when sawing.

▶ Ensure children know that they must not eat the berries.

Bibliography

[1] Moorhouse, Peter **All about woodwork** – article in Nursery World magazine, 14–27th May 2012 05-14

[2] **Common Sense, Common Safety** – Lord Young's report, September, 2010 (www.number10.gov.uk/)

Resources

Bag of nails – large, flat-headed nails available from Cosy Workshops 11 Empire Business Park, Parcel Terrace, Derby, DE1 1LY Tel 01332 370152 for catalogue (website in development at time of printing).

Blocks of rigid foam – available form Cosy Workshops

Range of tools – Child-sized, real tools available from TTS Early Years and Cosy Workshops

Short hammers – real, child-sized hammers available from Cosy Workshops

Softwood off-cuts – a larger than normal sack of softwood off-cuts are available from Cosy Workshops

Woodworking aprons, goggles and safety gloves – available from TTS Early Years and Cosy Workshops

Workbench – available from TTS Early Years and Cosy Workshops